A Benjamin Blog and his Inquisitive Dog Guide

KU-181-395

Russia

Anita Ganeri

SOUTHWARK LIBRARIES

SK 2579081 1

Raintree is an imprint of Capstone Global Library Limited, a company incorporated in England and Wales having its registered office at 7 Pilgrim Street, London, EC4V 6LB – Registered company number: 6695582

www.raintree.co.uk
myorders@raintree.co.uk

Text © Capstone Global Library Limited 2015
The moral rights of the proprietor have been asserted.

All rights reserved. No part of this publication may be reproduced in any form or by any means (including photocopying or storing it in any medium by electronic means and whether or not transiently or incidentally to some other use of this publication) without the written permission of the copyright owner, except in accordance with the provisions of the Copyright, Designs and Patents Act 1988 or under the terms of a licence issued by the Copyright Licensing Agency, Saffron House, 6–10 Kirby Street, London EC1N 8TS (www.cla.co.uk). Applications for the copyright owner's written permission should be addressed to the publisher.

Edited by Helen Cox Cannons
Designed by Philippa Jenkins and Tim Bond
Original illustrations © Capstone Global Library Limited 2015
Original map illustration by Oxford Designers and Illustrators
Ben and Barko Illustrated by Sernur ISIK
Picture research by Svetlana Zhurkin
Production by Helen McCreath
Originated by Capstone Global Library Limited
Printed and bound in China

ISBN 978 1 406 29837 6 (hardback)
19 18 17 16 15
10 9 8 7 6 5 4 3 2 1

ISBN 978 1 406 29842 0 (paperback)
20 19 18 17 16
10 9 8 7 6 5 4 3 2 1

British Library Cataloguing in Publication Data
A full catalogue record for this book is available from the British Library.

Acknowledgements
We would like to thank the following for permission to reproduce photographs: Alamy: Asia Photopress, 13, John Warburton-Lee Photography, 22; Dreamstime: Boris Akhunov, 15, Iakov Filimonov, 16; iStockphoto: Lara111, 24; Newscom: Zuma Press/ITAR-TASS/Vladimir Smirnov, 23, Zuma Press/Russian Look/Konstantin Mikhailov, 9; Shutterstock: Alex Alekseev, cover, Art Konovalov, 6, Dmitry Kosorukov, 18, Elena Shchipkova, 27, 29, Inna Felker, 14, Irina Afonskaya, 19, Jenoche, 17, MAR007, 21, mironov, 11, R3BV, 7, Serg Zastavkin, 10, Tatiana Grozetskaya, 26, trubach, 28, Valeriya Popova, 4, 12, withGod, 8; Svetlana Zhurkin, 20, 25.

Every effort has been made to contact copyright holders of material reproduced in this book. Any omissions will be rectified in subsequent printings if notice is given to the publisher.

All the internet addresses (URLs) given in this book were valid at the time of going to press. However, due to the dynamic nature of the internet, some addresses may have changed, or sites may have changed or ceased to exist since publication. While the author and publisher regret any inconvenience this may cause readers, no responsibility for any such changes can be accepted by either the author or the publisher.

Some words are shown in bold, **like this**. You can find out what they mean by looking in the glossary.

Contents

Welcome to Russia!

Hello! My name's Benjamin Blog and this is Barko Polo, my **inquisitive** dog. (He's named after ancient ace explorer **Marco Polo**.) We have just got back from our latest adventure – exploring Russia. We put this book together from some of the blog posts we wrote on the way.

Country borders

Arctic Ocean

N

SWEDEN
FINLAND
Baltic Sea
POLAND
ESTONIA
Lake Ladoga
LATVIA
■ **St Petersburg**
Lake Onega
LITHUANIA
BELARUS
■ **Moscow**
UKRAINE
Volga
Ural Mountains
Ob
Arctic Circle
RUSSIA
Irtysh
S I B E R I A
Lena
Yenisey
Amur
Black Sea
Caucasus Mts.
▲ *Mount Elbrus*
Lake Baikal
GEORGIA
ARMENIA
KAZAKHSTAN
AZERBAIJAN
Aral Sea
CHINA
Caspian Sea
MONGOLIA
NORTH KOREA
TURKMENISTAN
UZBEKISTAN
SOUTH KOREA
IRAN
Pacific Ocean
Kamchatka Peninsula
Kuril Islands
JAPAN

BARKO'S BLOG-TASTIC RUSSIA FACTS

Russia is the world's largest country. It is so huge that it stretches across two **continents** – Europe and Asia. It has borders with 14 other countries, and coastlines with the Arctic Ocean and Pacific Ocean.

The story of Russia

Posted by: Ben Blog | 7 June at 1.14 p.m.

Our tour began with a visit to St Petersburg. What a beautiful city this is. This is the spectacular Peterhof Palace, which was built by Peter the Great. He ruled Russia as **Tsar** then **emperor** from 1682 to 1725. During his reign, Russia became a huge and powerful empire.

BARKO'S BLOG-TASTIC RUSSIA FACTS

The Kremlin in Moscow is home to the Russian **president**. It is surrounded by high, red-brick walls and towers. Inside the Kremlin, there are four **gilt-domed** cathedrals and five grand palaces.

Lakes, rivers, forests and peaks

Posted by: Ben Blog | 2 July at 11.56 a.m.

From St Petersburg, we made the long journey south-east to Lake Baikal. At 1,642 metres (5,387 feet), it is the world's deepest lake. It is also one of the oldest, at 25 million years old. The lake is home to some amazing animals. These seals are the only seals that live in fresh water.

BARKO'S BLOG-TASTIC RUSSIA FACTS

There are more than 100,000 rivers in Russia. The longest is the River Lena, which flows for 4,399 kilometres (2,734 miles). It starts in the Baikal Mountains and flows to the Laptev Sea, part of the Arctic Ocean.

Heading north, we reached the taiga, a huge, **coniferous** forest that covers much of Siberia. Even further north, the forest thins out and there are enormous plains, known as tundra. Here, it is so cold that the ground stays frozen for much of the year. Brrrr!

BARKO'S BLOG-TASTIC RUSSIA FACTS

The Ural Mountains are a mighty mountain range that runs for around 2,500 kilometres (1,553 miles) from the north to the south of Russia. They form a boundary between Europe and Asia.

City tour

Our next stop was Moscow, the capital city of Russia. It is famous for St Basil's Cathedral, Red Square, the Kremlin and lots more besides. The best way to get about is by Metro (underground railway). We're here at Komsomolskaya station – look at those **chandeliers**!

BARKO'S BLOG-TASTIC RUSSIA FACTS

Vladivostok, in the far south-east, is one of Russia's most important cities. It is Russia's biggest **port** on the Pacific Ocean, and home to the Pacific Fleet (part of the Russian Navy).

Privet!

Most people in Russia speak Russian. *Privet!* (say "pree-VYET") means "Hi!" Russian is written in the Cyrillic alphabet. *Privet* is written like this [Привет!]. People in the different regions of Russia also speak their own local languages.

14

BARKO'S BLOG-TASTIC RUSSIA FACTS

More than 140 million people live in Russia. Most of them are Russians, but there are many other groups. These people are Tatars, wearing traditional dress. Tatars are Muslims and follow the religion of Islam.

In Russia, children start school when they are seven years old. Their first day at school is 1 September, which is called Knowledge Day. It is marked by a special assembly. The children dress up and carry bunches of flowers for the teachers. A bell rings to welcome them to the school.

BARKO'S BLOG-TASTIC RUSSIA FACTS

Most Russian people live in cities, in large apartment blocks. Most flats are quite small inside. In the countryside, many houses, churches and schools are made from wood.

Many Russian people belong to the Russian Orthodox Church. Back in Moscow, we're paying a visit to the magnificent Cathedral of Christ the Saviour. The Cathedral was destroyed in 1931 but was rebuilt in the 1990s. Thousands of people come here to worship.

BARKO'S BLOG-TASTIC RUSSIA FACTS

In February or March, Russians celebrate *Maslenitsa* (Pancake Week). There are snowball fights, sleigh rides, singing and dancing, and plenty of pancakes to eat.

Time for lunch...

All that sightseeing made us hungry, so we decided to stop for lunch. Russia is famous for its soup. I ordered a bowl of *borscht*, which is made from beetroot. You can eat it hot or cold, with a dollop of sour cream, a sprig of **dill** and a hunk of crusty rye bread.

BARKO'S BLOG-TASTIC RUSSIA FACTS

Blinis are thin pancakes, topped with butter, sour cream, jam or even caviar (fish eggs). The best caviar comes from fish called sturgeon, which live in the Caspian Sea, off western Russia.

21

Having fun

Our next stop was St Petersburg. We have tickets for the ballet at the Mariinsky Theatre. Russian ballet is famous around the world. We have come to watch the Mariinsky Ballet perform *Swan Lake*. This ballet tells the story of a princess who is turned into a swan.

BARKO'S BLOG-TASTIC RUSSIA FACTS

Sport is very popular in Russia. In 2014, the Winter Olympics were held in Sochi, in the south of Russia. The Russian team won the most medals – 13 gold, 11 silver and 9 bronze.

From drilling to dolls

Posted by: Ben Blog | 30 April at 10.25 a.m.

We're taking the famous Trans-Siberia railway through Siberia. This is where most of Russia's oil, coal, metals, diamonds and gold come from. The train transports huge loads of minerals from Siberia to western Russia. It is the longest railway line in the world.

BARKO'S BLOG-TASTIC RUSSIA FACTS

These Russian dolls are made from wood, and get smaller and smaller. They are placed inside each other, in order of size. In Russian, they are called *matryoshkas*.

25

And finally...

It is the last day of our trip, and we've travelled even further east to the Kamchatka Peninsula. I wanted to see the Valley of the **Geysers** where many geysers gush up from the ground. The only way to reach the Valley is by helicopter. Come on, Barko!

BARKO'S BLOG-TASTIC RUSSIA FACTS

St Basil's Cathedral in Red Square, Moscow, is the most famous building in Russia. It was built between 1555 and 1561, and has brightly painted onion-shaped **domes**. Amazing!

Russia fact file

Area: 17,098,200 square kilometres
(6,601,652 square miles)

Population: 143,700,000 (2014)

Capital city: Moscow

Other main cities: St Petersburg, Novosibirsk,
Vladivostok, Yekaterinburg

Language: Russian

Main religion: Christianity (Russian Orthodox)

Highest mountain: Mount Elbrus
(5,642 metres/18,510 feet)

Longest river: Lena (4,261 kilometres/2,648 miles)

Currency: Ruble

Russia quiz

Find out how much you know about Russia with our quick quiz.

1. How many countries have borders with Russia?
a) 4
b) 14
c) 24

2. Which is the deepest lake in the world?
a) Caspian Sea
b) Lake Superior
c) Lake Baikal

3. What does *Privet* mean?
a) Hi
b) Goodbye
c) How are you?

4. What is the main ingredient in *borscht*?
a) beetroot
b) cabbage
c) potatoes

5. What is this?

Answers
1. b
2. c
3. a
4. a
5. St Basil's Cathedral

Glossary

chandelier large, grand light that hangs from the ceiling

coniferous type of tree with needles instead of leaves that stays green all year round

continent large area of land

dill leafy herb

dome rounded top of a tower on a building

emperor ruler of a group of countries, called an empire

geyser jet of hot water that shoots up from under the ground

gilt gold-like paint or material

inquisitive interested in learning about the world

Marco Polo explorer who lived from about 1254 to 1324. He travelled from Italy to China.

port place where ships are loaded and unloaded

president head of a country that is a republic

Tsar name for the emperor of Russia before the year 1917

Find out more

Books

R is for Russia (World Alphabet), Vladimir Kabakov (Frances Lincoln, 2013)

Russia (Countries Around the World), Jilly Hunt (Raintree, 2013)

Russia (Countries in Our World), Galya Ransome (Franklin Watts, 2012)

Russia (Popcorn: Countries), Alice Harman (Wayland, 2013)

Websites

ngkids.co.uk
National Geographic's website has lots of information, photos and maps of countries around the world.

www.worldatlas.com
Packed with information about different countries, this website has flags, time zones, facts and figures, maps and timelines.

Index